KINGDOM DISCIPLESHIP SERIES BOOK 1

Foundational Studies for New Disciples

By
C Maurice Roxborough

New Generation Kingdom Movement
Copyright © 2024

TABLE OF CONTENTS

PREFACE

Welcome to the Kingdom of God!

N ow that you have made a decision to seek God's Kingdom and His Righteousness here are several things you will need to pay attention to. We like to call it the BRC/RFC Process: -

What must I do to enter the Kingdom of God? [BRC]

☐ **BELIEVE** – You can enter God's Kingdom **today** by **truly believing /trusting** in the person, life and works of **Jesus Christ!** God will **forgive you** of all your sins and give you **His new nature** helping you to **truly live** for Him!

So they said, "Believe on the Lord Jesus Christ, and you will be saved, you and your household." [Acts 16:31]

☐ **REPENT** – Many people claim to believe in Jesus but there is no evidence of this belief **bringing change** to their lives. This is faith that **cannot save**! A person who **truly believes** in the gospel will **also repent**! They will **turn from** their **sins** and **turn to God** in complete **obedience** to His words.

Repent therefore and be converted, that your sins may be blotted out, so that times of refreshing may come from the presence of the Lord... [Acts 3:19]

☐ **COMMIT** – Repentance is both a turn from sin and a turn to God in **true commitment**! In order to **escape sin** and be saved you will have to make the **decisions** and **sacrifices** to commit to the things of **God's Kingdom**! Below are three initial things you will **NEED** to commit to in order to be **successful** in your journey in the Kingdom of God!

And they continued steadfastly in the apostles' doctrine and fellowship, in the breaking of bread, and in prayers. [Acts 2:42]

What must I do to grow in the Kingdom of God? [RFC]

☐ **RELATIONSHIP** – Naturally you will have to **build** a **relationship** with God. This means you must **spend time** communicating with Him in **prayer consistently** as well as **reading His Word** to learn what pleases him!

And this is eternal life, that they may know You, the only true God, and Jesus Christ whom You have sent. [John 17:3]

☐ **FELLOWSHIP** – You will also have to build a **relationship** with the people of God – **the Church**! This means you should **make the time** to **attend** corporate **worship services regularly. Small group meetings** (e.g. Prayer and Bible studies) and **fellowship times** are also **very important**!

So continuing daily with one accord in the temple, and breaking bread from house to house, they ate their food with gladness and simplicity of heart... [Acts 2:46]

☐ **CONFESSION** – **Relationships** are **very influential** in your **life's direction**. You come into the Kingdom of God with relationships and friendships from the past. You **MUST CONFESS** your faith **to others** so that your decision to follow Christ will be **clear**! This will **strengthen your faith** while **challenging others** to pursue Jesus Christ and His Kingdom as well!

That if you confess with your mouth the Lord Jesus and believe in your heart that God has raised Him from the dead, you will be saved. [Romans 10:9]

DEDICATION

To my five children Joshua, Esther, Joelle Joy, Daniel and Joseph:

That your faith may be truly rooted and grounded in Jesus Christ!

SECTION 1

ENTERING THE KINGDOM OF GOD

But as many as received Him, to them He gave the right to become children of God, to those who believe in His name.
[John 1:12]

When we accept Jesus Christ as our Lord and Savior by believing and trusting in the work He has done to save us, God transforms us and makes us His children! He gives us a new birth into His glorious Kingdom where we can pursue Him and endeavor to learn His righteous way of living!

CHAPTER ONE

RESPONDING TO THE KINGDOM OF GOD

For after all these things the Gentiles seek. For your heavenly Father knows that you need all these things. But seek first the kingdom of God and His righteousness, and all these things shall be added to you. [Matthew 6:32 – 33]

The Kingdom of God is like a Great King who invited His guests to a banquet [Luke 14:15-24]. Everyone of these guests gave excuses why they could not attend and so they were therefore rejected! Their response to God's kingdom was totally wrong. In order to access God's Kingdom we must understand its great importance and therefore respond appropriately to its high priority demands on our daily lives. Here are several things we must learn about responding to the Kingdom of God!

- **We must understand the Great value of the kingdom of God!**

  "Again, the kingdom of heaven is like treasure hidden in a field, which a man found and hid; and for joy over it he goes and sells all that he has and buys that field. "Again, the kingdom of heaven is like a merchant seeking beautiful pearls, who, when he had found one pearl of great price, went and sold all that he had and bought it. [Matthew 13:44 – 46]

- **We must therefore esteem God's Kingdom as number one priority in our lives!**

  But seek first the kingdom of God and His righteousness, and all these things shall be added to you. [Matthew 6:33]

  "The law and the prophets were until John. Since that time the kingdom of God has been preached, and everyone is pressing into it. [Luke 16:16]

- **We must give up all, take up our Cross and follow Christ even at the expense of our own lives!!!**

  Then He said to them all, "If anyone desires to come after Me, let him deny himself, and take up his cross daily, and follow Me. [Luke 9:23]

  "If anyone comes to Me and does not hate his father and mother, wife and children, brothers and sisters, yes, and his own life also, he cannot be My disciple... So likewise, whoever of you does not forsake all that he has cannot be My disciple. [Luke 14:26, 33]

- **We should repent of our old sinful lifestyle and submit ourselves to the radical life transformation of the Kingdom of God!**

  In those days John the Baptist came preaching in the wilderness of Judea and saying, "Repent, for the kingdom of heaven is at hand!" [Matthew 3:1, 2]

  And do not be conformed to this world, but be transformed by the renewing of your mind, that you may prove what is that good and acceptable and perfect will of God. [Romans 12:2]

- **We must realize that the Kingdom of God is the only means of executing the Love of God to reach the lost and dying world!**

  For God so loved the world that He gave His only begotten Son, that whoever believes in Him should not perish but have everlasting life. [John 3:16]

  Then Jesus went about all the cities and villages, teaching in their synagogues, preaching the gospel of the kingdom, and healing every sickness and every disease among the people. But when He saw the multitudes, He was moved with compassion for them, because they were weary and scattered, like sheep having no shepherd. Then He said to His disciples, "The harvest truly is plentiful, but the laborers are few. Therefore pray the Lord of the harvest to send out laborers into His harvest." [Matthew 9:35 –38]

  And when He had called His twelve disciples to Him, He gave them power over unclean spirits, to cast them out, and to heal all kinds of sickness and all kinds of disease. [Matthew 10: 1]

Reflective Questions

Answer the following questions giving reasons where necessary

1. How important is the Kingdom of God to you?
   ☐Very important
   ☐Somewhat important
   ☐Not really important

   Why is this so?

2. What are you willing to do to show how much you value the kingdom of God?
   ☐Give up everything for God
   ☐Surrender my life to God's change
   ☐Follow in Jesus' footsteps

3. As a part of the Kingdom of God, how do you think we can show the love of God to a lost and dying world?

CHAPTER TWO

REPENTANCE

Repent therefore and be converted, that your sins may be blotted out, so that times of refreshing may come from the presence of the Lord... [Acts 3:19]

Repentance

To 'repent' means to *change one's mind or thinking*! A change of mind will always result in a change of action; so true faith in Jesus will always result in a change of lifestyle! When we leave the kingdom of darkness and come into the kingdom of light and of God, we have to abandon the old way of thinking and doing things and learn God's way of thinking and doing things!

Here are five things you should learn about biblical repentance:

- **Repentance is the first response to the Kingdom of God! God calls and gives every human being the potential to repent!**

  From that time Jesus began to preach and to say, "Repent, for the kingdom of heaven is at hand."
  [Matthew 4:17]

  Truly, these times of ignorance God overlooked, but now commands all men everywhere to repent...
  [Acts 17:30]

- **Repentance involves confessing our sins, turning from them and turning to God!**

  He who covers his sins will not prosper, But whoever confesses and forsakes them will have mercy.
  [Proverbs 28:13]

  Let the wicked forsake his way, And the unrighteous man his thoughts; Let him return to the LORD, And He will have mercy on him; And to our God, For He will abundantly pardon. [Isaiah 55:7]

- **Repentance, where possible, sometimes involves restitution and reconciliation!**

  And Zacchaeus stood, and said unto the Lord: Behold, Lord, the half of my goods I give to the poor; and if I have taken any thing from any man by false accusation, I restore him fourfold. [Luke 19:8]

  Therefore if thou bring thy gift to the altar, and there rememberest that thy brother hath ought against thee;

Leave there thy gift before the altar, and go thy way; first be reconciled to thy brother, and then come and offer thy gift. [Matthew 5:23-24]

- **God promises to forgive our sins and save us if we repent!**
Repent therefore and be converted, that your sins may be blotted out, so that times of refreshing may come from the presence of the Lord... [Acts 3:19]

If we confess our sins, He is faithful and just to forgive us our sins and to cleanse us from all unrighteousness. [1 John 1:9]

- **Repentance involves a continuous renewal of the mind by the Word of God!**
And do not be conformed to this world, but be transformed by the renewing of your mind, that you may prove what is that good and acceptable and perfect will of God. [Romans 12:2]

But you have not so learned Christ, if indeed you have heard Him and have been taught by Him, as the truth is in Jesus: that you put off, concerning your former conduct, the old man which grows corrupt according to the deceitful lusts, and be renewed in the spirit of your mind, and that you put on the new man which was created according to God, in true righteousness and holiness. [Ephesians 4: 20 – 24]

Reflective Questions

Answer the following questions giving reasons where necessary

1. Do you desire to enter the Kingdom of God?

   _____

   _____

   _____

   _____

   _____

   _____

2. Have you repented of your sins? Tick which of the following you have done:
   - ☐ Confessed them to God
   - ☐ Turned away from them
   - ☐ Turn to God in a New way of life

3. Do you think that restitution and restoration might be applicable in your situation? Explain

   _____

   _____

   _____

   _____

   _____

   _____

CHAPTER THREE

NEW BIRTH

Therefore if any man be in Christ, he is a new creature: old things are passed away; behold, all things are become new.
[2 Corinthians 5:17]

The Bible teaches us that God's standards for His Kingdom are very high! No normal human being can fulfill the requirements of God's Kingdom! So in order for us to enter God's Kingdom and live up to its requirements we must be transformed into nothing less than super-human! And this is what He promises to make us when we enter into His Holy Kingdom!!! Here are a few things we can learn about being born into the Kingdom of God: -

- **We were all born in the kingdom of sin therefore we MUST experience spiritual rebirth before we can see (understand) or enter the Kingdom of God!**

Behold, I was brought forth in iniquity, And in sin my mother conceived me. [Psalm 51:5]

Jesus answered and said to him, "Most assuredly, I say to you, unless one is born again, he cannot see the kingdom of God." Do not marvel that I said to you, 'You must be born again.' [John 3:3, 7]

- **God is the only one who can grant us new birth!**
He came to His own, and His own did not receive Him. But as many as received Him, to them He gave the right to become children of God, to those who believe in His name: who were born, not of blood, nor of the will of the flesh, nor of the will of man, but of God. [John 1: 11 – 13]

- **Our role in the process of being born again is to truly believe in Jesus Christ and repent of our sins! This serious decision is symbolic in our baptism!**
And He said to them, "Go into all the world and preach the gospel to every creature. He that believeth and is baptized shall be saved; but he that believeth not shall be damned. [Mark 16:15, 16]

Then Peter said to them, "Repent, and let every one of you be baptized in the name of Jesus Christ for the remission of sins; and you shall receive the gift of the Holy Spirit. [Acts 2:38]

- **God grants new birth to those who truly believe and repent by the washing of their sins by the blood (the**

water) and the indwelling of His Holy Spirit (the spirit).

Jesus answered, "Most assuredly, I say to you, unless one is born of water and the Spirit, he cannot enter the kingdom of God. [John 3:5]

... Not by works of righteousness which we have done, but according to His mercy He saved us, through the washing of regeneration and renewing of the Holy Spirit... [Titus 3:5]

- **As children of God we will face temptation, persecution and suffering but we must always remember that everyone who experiences new birth has overcome sin, satan and the world!**
And when they had preached the gospel to that city and made many disciples, they returned to Lystra, Iconium, and Antioch, strengthening the souls of the disciples, exhorting them to continue in the faith, and saying, "We must through many tribulations enter the kingdom of God." [Acts 14:21, 22]

Whoever has been born of God does not sin, for His seed remains in him; and he cannot sin, because he has been born of God... You are of God, little children, and have overcome them, because He who is in you is greater than he who is in the world... For whatever is born of God overcomes the world. And this is the victory that has overcome the world—our faith. [1 John 3:9, 4:4, 5:4]

Reflective Questions

Answer the following questions giving reasons where necessary

1. Have you truly believed in Jesus Christ and have repented of your sins?

   _____

   _____

   _____

   _____

   _____

2. Since then have you sense that God has made a special change in your life? Explain

   _____

   _____

   _____

   _____

   _____

   _____

3. Do you think that living for the Kingdom of God will be easy? How do you think you will endure?

   _____

   _____

   _____

   _____

   _____

CHAPTER FOUR

BAPTISM

Go ye therefore, and teach all nations, baptizing them in the name of the Father, and of the Son, and of the Holy Ghost: Teaching them to observe all things whatsoever I have commanded you: and, lo, I am with you always, even unto the end of the world. Amen. [Matthew 28:19, 20]

Baptism

The word 'baptism' comes from a Greek word which means to *dip or submerge*. When we are baptized we identify with Christ as our Lord, Savior and King. Just as he died, was buried and raised to life again; so we symbolize through our baptism that we died to sin, have buried the old way of life and are now created new; to live like Christ!

Here are a few things we should know about baptism.

- **If we truly believe in Jesus Christ and repent of our sins we should be baptized!**

  And He said to them, "Go into all the world and preach the gospel to every creature. He that believeth and is baptized shall be saved; but he that believeth not shall be damned. [Mark 16:15, 16]

  Then Peter said to them, "Repent, and let every one of you be baptized in the name of Jesus Christ for the remission of sins; and you shall receive the gift of the Holy Spirit. [Acts 2:38]

- **Baptism symbolizes our death to sin, burial of the old sinful lifestyle and resurrection to new life in Christ!**

  Or do you not know that as many of us as were baptized into Christ Jesus were baptized into His death? Therefore we were buried with Him through baptism into death, that just as Christ was raised from the dead by the glory of the Father, even so we also should walk in newness of life. [Romans 6:3, 4]

  In Him you were also circumcised with the circumcision made without hands, by putting off the body of the sins of the flesh, by the circumcision of Christ, buried with Him in baptism, in which you also were raised with Him through faith in the working of God, who raised Him from the dead. [Colossians 2:11, 12]

- **Baptism is a symbol; it cannot wash away our sins or save us! It is true faith in Jesus Christ that saves us!**

  For by grace you have been saved through faith, and that not of yourselves; it is the gift of God, not of works, lest anyone should boast. [Ephesians 2:8, 9]

  There is also an antitype which now saves us—baptism (not the removal of the filth of the flesh, but the answer of a good conscience toward God), through the resurrection of Jesus Christ... [1 Peter 3:21]

- **Baptism demonstrates our commitment to become true disciples of Christ!**
  Go therefore and make disciples of all the nations, baptizing them in the name of the Father and of the Son and of the Holy Spirit... [Matthew 28:19]

  Then Jesus came from Galilee to John at the Jordan to be baptized by him. And John tried to prevent Him, saying, "I need to be baptized by You, and are You coming to me?" But Jesus answered and said to him, "Permit it to be so now, for thus it is fitting for us to fulfill all righteousness." Then he allowed Him. When He had been baptized, Jesus came up immediately from the water; and behold, the heavens were opened to Him, and He saw the Spirit of God descending like a dove and alighting upon Him. And suddenly a voice came from heaven, saying, "This is My beloved Son, in whom I am well pleased." [Matthew 3:13 – 17]

25

Reflective Questions

Answer the following questions giving reasons where necessary

1. Do you truly believe in Jesus and want to be his true disciple?

   _____

   _____

   _____

   _____

2. Do you want to be baptized to show your true commitment to be His disciple? Why? Why not?

   _____

   _____

   _____

   _____

   _____

   _____

3. Do you have to be baptized to enter the Kingdom of God? What does baptism mean?

   _____

   _____

   _____

   _____

   _____

   _____

SECTION 2

GROWING IN YOUR RELATIONSHIP WITH GOD!

But we will give ourselves continually to prayer, and to the ministry of the word. [Acts 6:4]

Building a relationship with Jesus through the Holy Spirit and learning to walk with Him is a critical part of being a disciple of Christ! In order to do this effectively you will need to learn how to spend quality time in prayer and the Word of God – the Bible!

CHAPTER FIVE

PRAYER

And take the helmet of salvation, and the sword of the Spirit, which is the word of God; praying always with all prayer and supplication in the Spirit, being watchful to this end with all perseverance and supplication for all the saints— [Ephesians 6:17, 18]

Prayer

Prayer can be defined simply as *'spiritual communication'*! Communication is vital to building and maintaining a close relationship with loved ones. This applies also to the Divine Person of God manifested to us in the Holy Spirit now living within us! We must walk with Him, talk with Him, laugh with Him, consult Him, listen to and obey Him daily!

Here are some important keys to prayer:

- **As children of God we must pray to God the Father in Jesus name!**
  But you, when you pray, go into your room, and when you have shut your door, pray to your Father who is in the secret place; and your Father who sees in secret will reward you openly. [Matthew 6:6]

  And whatever you ask in My name, that I will do, that the Father may be glorified in the Son. If you ask anything in My name, I will do it. [John 14:13, 14]

- **As Christ's disciples we must set aside a suitable time and place to meet with God regularly in prayer!**
  Now in the morning, having risen a long while before daylight, He went out and departed to a solitary place; and there He prayed. [Mark 1:35]

  Who, in the days of His flesh, when He had offered up prayers and supplications, with vehement cries and tears to Him who was able to save Him from death, and was heard because of His godly fear... [Hebrews 5:7]

- **We must be devoted to prayer; praying constantly throughout the day – wherever whenever!**
  Continue earnestly in prayer, being vigilant in it with thanksgiving... [Colossians 4:2]
  Pray without ceasing... [1 Thessalonians 5:17]

- **If we pray we will be saved from temptation!**

And do not lead us into temptation, But deliver us from the evil one. For Yours is the kingdom and the power and the glory forever. Amen. Watch and pray, lest you enter into temptation. The spirit indeed is willing, but the flesh is weak." [Matthew 6:13, 26:41]

- **Some keys to effective prayer are that it must be full of faith, fervent and bold in our righteousness in Christ!**
  Therefore I say to you, whatever things you ask when you pray, believe that you receive them, and you will have them. [Mark 11:24]

  Confess your trespasses to one another, and pray for one another, that you may be healed. The effective, fervent prayer of a righteous man avails much. [James 5:16]

Reflective Questions

Answer the following questions giving reasons where necessary

1. What do you think about the fact that God is a person just like us?

    _____

    _____

    _____

    _____

    _____

2. Have you set aside a suitable time and place to meet with God in prayer?

    _____

    _____

    _____

    _____

    _____

3. How committed have you been to prayer in your daily life recently?

    _____

    _____

    _____

    _____

    _____

CHAPTER SIX

THE WORD OF GOD

Study to shew thyself approved unto God, a workman that needeth not to be ashamed, rightly dividing the word of truth. [2 Timothy 2:15]

The Word of God

The Word of God – the Bible, came to us through the faithful writings of 40 different writers from varying time periods, ages, occupations and backgrounds over a span of 2500 years. The Bible stands alone in its uniqueness – it is the most read, printed, studied, circulated, translated (to other languages), written about, quoted, controversial and also shoplifted book of all times! Astounding prophecies, remarkable coherency and preservation, archaeological and historical accuracy as well as scientific insights well beyond the time of its documentation set the

Bible apart as not just unique but as the divinely inspired Word of God! Here's what the Bible has to say about itself:

- **The Bible is the inspired Word of God! Men did not write what they wanted but were *directed by God's Holy Spirit*!**

  All Scripture is given by inspiration of God, and is profitable for doctrine, for reproof, for correction, for instruction in righteousness... [2 Timothy 3:16]

  knowing this first, that no prophecy of Scripture is of any private interpretation, for prophecy never came by the will of man, but holy men of God spoke as they were moved by the Holy Spirit. [2 Peter 1: 20, 21]

- **God's Words are alive and powerful! They create and sustain the whole universe!**

  Who being the brightness of His glory and the express image of His person, and upholding all things by the word of His power, when He had by Himself purged our sins, sat down at the right hand of the Majesty on high... for the word of God is living and powerful, and sharper than any two-edged sword, piercing even to the division of soul and spirit, and of joints and marrow, and is a discerner of the thoughts and intents of the heart... By faith we understand that the worlds were framed by the word of God, so that the things which are seen were not made of things which are visible. [Hebrews 1:3, 4:12, 11:3]

- **As milk is critical to a new born baby, so the Word of God is critical to a new disciple in Christ! It is also meat and solid food for the mature disciple!**
  As newborn babes, desire the pure milk of the word, that you may grow thereby... [1 Peter 2:2]

  For though by this time you ought to be teachers, you need someone to teach you again the first principles of the oracles of God; and you have come to need milk and not solid food. For everyone who partakes only of milk is unskilled in the word of righteousness, for he is a babe. But solid food belongs to those who are of full age, that is, those who by reason of use have their senses exercised to discern both good and evil. [Hebrews 5:12 – 14]

- **The Word of God will empower us to overcome the devil and remain pure!**
  How can a young man cleanse his way? By taking heed according to Your word... Your word I have hidden in my heart, That I might not sin against You. [Psalm 119:9, 11]

  But he answered and said, It is written, Man shall not live by bread alone, but by every word that proceedeth out of the mouth of God... Jesus said unto him, It is written again, Thou shalt not tempt the Lord thy God... Then saith Jesus unto him, Get thee hence, Satan: for it is written, Thou shalt worship the Lord thy God, and him only shalt thou serve. [Matthew 4:4, 7, 10]

- **God promises to bless us if we take quality time to study, meditate and apply the Word of God to our lives!**

  But his delight is in the law of the LORD, And in His law he meditates day and night. He shall be like a tree Planted by the rivers of water, That brings forth its fruit in its season, Whose leaf also shall not wither; And whatever he does shall prosper. [Psalm 1:2, 3]

  Only be strong and very courageous, that you may observe to do according to all the law which Moses My servant commanded you; do not turn from it to the right hand or to the left, that you may prosper wherever you go. This Book of the Law shall not depart from your mouth, but you shall meditate in it day and night, that you may observe to do according to all that is written in it. For then you will make your way prosperous, and then you will have good success. [Joshua 1:7, 8]

Reflective Questions

Answer the following questions giving reasons where necessary

1. Do you believe the Bible is the inspired Word of God? Why or why not?

   _____

   _____

   _____

   _____

   _____

2. Have you started to read your Bible regularly? How regularly?

   _____

   _____

   _____

   _____

   _____

3. How do you think the Word of God can help you to overcome sin & temptation?

   _____

   _____

   _____

   _____

   _____

CHAPTER SEVEN
WORSHIP

Wherefore we receiving a kingdom which cannot be moved, let us have grace, whereby we may serve [worship] God acceptably with reverence and godly fear: For our God is a consuming fire. [Hebrews 12:28, 29, insertion added]

Worship

Worship is the act of *being and showing submission to God*! Anything we do to demonstrate our obedience and submission to God can therefore be defined as worship! Worship therefore goes far beyond singing songs in a meeting – worship should be a continuous lifestyle before God! Our greatest form of worship therefore is offering our bodies as living sacrifices, holy and acceptable to God! As the Bible declares: 'Worship the Lord in the beauty of Holiness' [1 Chronicles 16:29]!

Here are some key facts about worship:

- **Worship should be centered on God not on anything else!**
  Then Jesus said to him, "Away with you, Satan! For it is written, 'You shall worship the LORD your God, and Him only you shall serve." [Matthew 4:10]

  Around the throne were twenty-four thrones, and on the thrones I saw twenty-four elders sitting, clothed in white robes; and they had crowns of gold on their heads... The twenty-four elders fall down before Him who sits on the throne and worship Him who lives forever and ever, and cast their crowns before the throne, saying; Thou art worthy, O Lord, to receive glory and honour and power: for thou hast created all things, and for thy pleasure they are and were created. [Revelations 4:4, 10, 11]

- **Worship should be acceptable to God in reverential fear and awe; based on His holy standards and not our own!**
  Therefore, since we are receiving a kingdom which cannot be shaken, let us have grace, by which we may serve God acceptably with reverence and godly fear. [Hebrews 12:28]

  For from the rising of the sun, even to its going down, My name shall be great among the Gentiles; In every place incense shall be offered to My name, And a pure offering; For My name shall be great among the nations," Says the

LORD of hosts. "But you profane it, In that you say, 'The table of the LORD is defiled; And its fruit, its food, is contemptible.' You also say, 'Oh, what a weariness!' And you sneer at it," Says the LORD of hosts. "And you bring the stolen, the lame, and the sick; Thus you bring an offering! Should I accept this from your hand?" Says the LORD. "But cursed be the deceiver Who has in his flock a male, And takes a vow, But sacrifices to the Lord what is blemished— For I am a great King," Says the LORD of hosts, "And My name is to be feared among the nations. [Malachi 1:11 – 14]*

- **Worship should be sincerely from the heart and not based on lip-service or other externals!**
  This people draweth nigh unto me with their mouth, and honoureth me with their lips; but their heart is far from me. [Matthew 15:8]

  But the hour is coming, and now is, when the true worshipers will worship the Father in spirit and truth; for the Father is seeking such to worship Him. God is Spirit, and those who worship Him must worship in spirit and truth." [John 4:23, 24]

- **Worship should be our best offering; it should be a sacrifice that costs us something!**
  And in the process of time it came to pass that Cain brought an offering of the fruit of the ground to the LORD. Abel also brought of the firstborn of his flock and of their fat. And the LORD respected Abel and his offering, but He did not respect Cain and his offering. And Cain was very angry, and his countenance fell. [Genesis 4:3 – 5]

Then the king said to Araunah, "No, but I will surely buy it from you for a price; nor will I offer burnt offerings to the LORD my God with that which costs me nothing." So David bought the threshing floor and the oxen for fifty shekels of silver. [2 Samuel 24:24]

- **Worship should be a holy life of sacrifice and surrender to God!**
  I beseech you therefore, brethren, by the mercies of God, that you present your bodies a living sacrifice, holy, acceptable to God, which is your reasonable service. [Romans 12:1]

Reflective Questions

Answer the following questions giving reasons where necessary:

1. Have you been cultivating a lifestyle of true worship before God?

   _____
   _____
   _____
   _____
   _____

2. Have you been living in obedience and submission to God's daily leadership through the Holy Spirit?

   _____
   _____
   _____
   _____
   _____

3. What do you think you need to do in order to attain a greater place of true worship before God?

   _____
   _____
   _____
   _____
   _____

CHAPTER EIGHT

FELLOWSHIP

*And they, continuing daily with one accord in the temple,
and breaking bread from house to house, did eat their meat
with gladness and singleness of heart...*
[Acts 2:46]

Fellowship

Fellowship is a key ingredient to the disciple's growth and development in the Kingdom of God. As every new born baby needs a family to love, care for and train them, so every new disciple needs a spiritual family to do just the same! Fellowship is more than just a group of people meeting together; fellowship is *believers dwelling together in love and unity, knitted together around the Word of God – the Bible*! One of God's greatest desires is for His Church to be in true fellowship with Him and with each other. There are multiple benefits to such a relationship in the Kingdom, the following are just a few:

- **True fellowship can only be achieved when all the believers endeavor to walk in the Light of Christ by obeying His Word!**

  That which we have seen and heard we declare to you, that you also may have fellowship with us; and truly our fellowship is with the Father and with His Son Jesus Christ. And these things we write to you that your joy may be full. This is the message which we have heard from Him and declare to you, that God is light and in Him is no darkness at all. If we say that we have fellowship with Him, and walk in darkness, we lie and do not practice the truth. But if we walk in the light as He is in the light, we have fellowship with one another, and the blood of Jesus Christ His Son cleanses us from all sin... By this we know that we love the children of God, when we love God and keep His commandments. [1 John 1:3 – 7, 5:2]

- **When we continually remain in true fellowship it keeps us 'sharpened' – focused, encouraged and strong!**

  As iron sharpens iron, So a man sharpens the countenance of his friend. [Proverbs 27:17]

  Not forsaking the assembling of ourselves together, as is the manner of some, but exhorting one another, and so much the more as you see the Day approaching. [Hebrews 10:25]

- **True fellowship empowers us to effectively help each other while protecting us from the attacks of the enemy!**

  Be sober, be vigilant; because your adversary the devil walks about like a roaring lion, seeking whom he may devour. Resist him, steadfast in the faith, knowing that the same sufferings are experienced by your brotherhood in the world. [1Peter 5:8, 9]

  Resist him, steadfast in the faith, knowing that the same sufferings are experienced by your brotherhood in the world. [Galatians 6:1, 2]

  Confess your trespasses to one another, and pray for one another, that you may be healed. The effective, fervent prayer of a righteous man avails much. [James 5:16]

- **When we walk in true fellowship the Body of Christ will be able to have greater impact!**

  Five of you shall chase a hundred, and a hundred of you shall put ten thousand to flight; your enemies shall fall by the sword before you. [Leviticus 26:8]

  "Again I say to you that if two of you agree on earth concerning anything that they ask, it will be done for them by My Father in heaven. [Matthew 18:19]

  And the LORD said, "Indeed the people are one and they all have one language, and this is what they begin to do; now nothing that they propose to do will be withheld from them. [Genesis 11:6]

44

- **God commands a blessing on the true fellowship of believers!**

    Behold, how good and how pleasant it is for brethren to dwell together in unity! It is like the precious oil upon the head, running down on the beard, the beard of Aaron, running down on the edge of his garments. It is like the dew of Hermon, descending upon the mountains of Zion; for there the LORD commanded the blessing—Life forevermore. [Psalm 133]

Reflective Questions

Answer the following questions giving reasons where necessary

1. Have you been dwelling in true fellowship with the Body of believers – the Church?

   _____

   _____

   _____

   _____

   _____

2. What are some of the benefits of walking in true fellowship with our fellow believers in Christ?

   _____

   _____

   _____

   _____

   _____

3. What are some of the areas of fellowship that you need to improve on? How will you work on these areas?

   _____

   _____

   _____

   _____

   _____

SECTION 3

GETTING PREPARED FOR SERVICE!

Now all things are of God, who has reconciled us to Himself through Jesus Christ, and has given us the ministry of reconciliation... [2 Corinthians 5:18]

As we grow in maturity and in our knowledge of God, there is an expectation as disciples that we should be prepared to serve. Though everyone is not called to be an Elder in the Church, all are expected to endeavor in Christ to become mature ministers of the Gospel of the Kingdom!

CHAPTER NINE

HOLINESS

But now being made free from sin, and become servants to God, ye have your fruit unto holiness, and the end everlasting life. [Romans 6:22]

Holiness

Holiness comes from God; the Scriptures refer to God as the Holy One of Israel [Isaiah 43:15]! When we received Christ we received the Spirit of Holiness who enables us to live up to God's holy standards. This happens as we subdue the flesh and walk in obedience to the dictates of the Spirit through a renewed mind that is continuously being transformed by the Word of God. [Ephesians 4:22 - 24]. Holiness means *to be set apart* and God makes us holy or set apart when we consecrate ourselves to Him for His use only!   Holiness makes us uncommon; possessing a clear distinction in purity, excellence and superiority!

- **The Bible calls us a Holy Nation and Royal priesthood; set apart from the world in word, deed and lifestyle!**

  And what agreement has the temple of God with idols? For you are the temple of the living God. As God has said: "I will dwell in them And walk among them. I will be their God, And they shall be My people." Therefore "Come out from among them And be separate, says the Lord. Do not touch what is unclean, And I will receive you." "I will be a Father to you, And you shall be My sons and daughters, Says the Lord Almighty."

  [2 Corinthians 6:16 – 18]

  But you are a chosen generation, a royal priesthood, a holy nation, His own special people, that you may proclaim the praises of Him who called you out of darkness into His marvelous light... [1 Peter 2:9]

- **Since God is Holy, as children and sons of God we should reflect His holy nature and character!**

  In the year that King Uzziah died, I saw the Lord sitting on a throne, high and lifted up, and the train of His robe filled the temple. Above it stood seraphim; each one had six wings: with two he covered his face, with two he covered his feet, and with two he flew. And one cried to another and said: "Holy, holy, holy is the Lord of hosts; The whole earth is full of His glory!" [Isaiah 6:1 – 3]

But as He who called you is holy, you also be holy in all your conduct, because it is written, "Be holy, for I am holy." [1 Peter 1:15, 16]

Pursue peace with all people, and holiness, without which no one will see the Lord... [Hebrews 12:14]

- **Ministry with power and giftedness is good, but God desires a lifestyle of humility, holiness and obedience above all else!**

  "Not everyone who says to Me, 'Lord, Lord,' shall enter the kingdom of heaven, but he who does the will of My Father in heaven. Many will say to Me in that day, 'Lord, Lord, have we not prophesied in Your name, cast out demons in Your name, and done many wonders in Your name?' And then I will declare to them, 'I never knew you; depart from Me, you who practice lawlessness!' [Matthew 7: 21 – 23]

  Nevertheless the solid foundation of God stands, having this seal: "The Lord knows those who are His," and, "Let everyone who names the name of Christ depart from iniquity." [2 Timothy 2:19]

- **God has supplied us with everything we need to live for Him in Holiness through the indwelling Holy Spirit!**

  For the grace of God that brings salvation has appeared to all men, teaching us that, denying ungodliness and worldly lusts, we should live soberly, righteously, and godly in the present age... [Titus 2:11, 12]

As His divine power has given to us all things that pertain to life and godliness, through the knowledge of Him who called us by glory and virtue... [2 Peter 1:3]

- **As people of God if we keep on sinning we put God to open disgrace and store up for ourselves God's judgment and wrath!**

  For if we sin willfully after we have received the knowledge of the truth, there no longer remains a sacrifice for sins, but a certain fearful expectation of judgment, and fiery indignation which will devour the adversaries. Anyone who has rejected Moses' law dies without mercy on the testimony of two or three witnesses. Of how much worse punishment, do you suppose, will he be thought worthy who has trampled the Son of God underfoot, counted the blood of the covenant by which he was sanctified a common thing, and insulted the Spirit of grace? [Hebrews 10:26 – 29]

  But in accordance with your hardness and your impenitent heart you are treasuring up for yourself wrath in the day of wrath and revelation of the righteous judgment of God... [Romans 2:5]

Reflective Questions

Answer the following questions giving reasons where necessary

1. What do you think of the fact that as a disciple of Christ you are made Holy by the indwelling Holy Spirit?

2. Have you been living a life of holiness – set apart for God's use only?

   _____

   _____

   _____

   _____

   _____

3. What do you think you need to do in order to attain a greater place of holiness in God?

   _____

   _____

   _____

   _____

   _____

CHAPTER TEN

DISCIPLESHIP

And he said to them all, If any man will come after me, let him deny himself, and take up his cross daily, and follow me. [Luke 9:23]

Discipleship

True fellowship creates the atmosphere for discipleship. The decision to accept Christ and His Kingdom is also a decision to follow Him as his disciple! When Jesus called His disciples to follow Him, He meant more than just following Him around. The call to discipleship literally means to *abandon one's old way of life and to now learn and imitate the lifestyle of Christ* as you walk with him daily! To be able to do this we must be trained in our personal lives by obedience to the Holy Spirit. We must also be mentored by the five-fold leaders Christ has appointed in His Church [Ephesians 4:11-14].

Here are a few things we must learn about accepting the call to follow Christ as disciples:

- **Following Jesus means loving Him more than everyone, everything and even your own life!**
  But he who denies Me before men will be denied before the angels of God... "If anyone comes to Me and does not hate his father and mother, wife and children, brothers and sisters, yes, and his own life also, he cannot be My disciple. [Luke 12:9, 14:26]

- **To follow Christ necessitates that we give up everything for Him!**
  From that time Jesus began to preach and to say, "Repent, for the kingdom of heaven is at hand." And Jesus, walking by the Sea of Galilee, saw two brothers, Simon called Peter, and Andrew his brother, casting a net into the sea; for they were fishermen. Then He said to them, "Follow Me, and I will make you fishers of men." They immediately left their nets and followed Him. Going on from there, He saw two other brothers, James the son of Zebedee, and John his brother, in the boat with Zebedee their father, mending their nets. He called them, and immediately they left the boat and their father, and followed Him. [Matthew 4:17 – 22]

  So likewise, whoever of you does not forsake all that he has cannot be My disciple. [Luke 14:33]

- **To be a true disciple of Christ we must bear the fruits of Christ's true Character!**

Herein is my Father glorified, that ye bear much fruit; so shall ye be my disciples... By this all will know that you are My disciples, if you have love for one another." [John 15:8, 13:35]

Ye shall know them by their fruits. Do men gather grapes of thorns, or figs of thistles? Even so every good tree bringeth forth good fruit; but a corrupt tree bringeth forth evil fruit. A good tree cannot bring forth evil fruit, neither can a corrupt tree bring forth good fruit. [Matthew 7:16-18]

- **Following Christ means manifesting the same works He did on earth!**

  "Most assuredly, I say to you, he who believes in Me, the works that I do he will do also; and greater works than these he will do, because I go to My Father. [John 14:12]

  He who believes and is baptized will be saved; but he who does not believe will be condemned. And these signs will follow those who believe: In My name they will cast out demons; they will speak with new tongues; they will take up serpents; and if they drink anything deadly, it will by no means hurt them; they will lay hands on the sick, and they will recover." [Mark 16: 15 – 18]

- **Being a disciple of Christ means reaping the abundant blessings of Christ in this life as well as in the life to come!**

  "Again, the kingdom of heaven is like treasure hidden in a field, which a man found and hid; and for joy over it he

goes and sells all that he has and buys that field. "Again, the kingdom of heaven is like a merchant seeking beautiful pearls, who, when he had found one pearl of great price, went and sold all that he had and bought it.
[Matthew 13:44 – 46]

Then Peter began to say to Him, "See, we have left all and followed You." So Jesus answered and said, "Assuredly, I say to you, there is no one who has left house or brothers or sisters or father or mother or wife or children or lands, for My sake and the gospel's, who shall not receive a hundredfold now in this time—houses and brothers and sisters and mothers and children and lands, with persecutions—and in the age to come, eternal life. [Mark 10:28 – 30]

Reflective Questions

Answer the following questions giving reasons where necessary

1. Have you been answering the call to follow Christ in your daily lives? How would you rate (out of 10) your daily obedience to discipleship?

   _____
   _____
   _____
   _____
   _____

2. How have you been demonstrating your life of discipleship:
   - ☐ Giving up & surrendering everything to Christ
   - ☐ Denying myself and taking up my cross daily
   - ☐ Loving Jesus more than everything, everyone and even my own life!

3. What do you need to do in order to improve your daily discipleship in Christ?

   _____
   _____
   _____
   _____
   _____

CHAPTER ELEVEN

THE HOLY SPIRIT

But the Comforter, which is the Holy Ghost, whom the Father will send in my name, he shall teach you all things, and bring all things to your remembrance, whatsoever I have said unto you. [John 14:26]

The Holy Spirit

The Holy Spirit is called *the Comforter and Counselor*. He is the Person of God sent by Jesus Christ, after His ascension, to continue the work of 'comforting' and 'counseling' His disciples on earth! He serves as Governor of the Kingdom of God on earth as well as Chief 'discipler'; equipping and empowering the believers in Christ. Here are a few things you should learn about the precious Holy Spirit:

- **The Holy Spirit convicts us of sin so that we may turn to God!**

Nevertheless I tell you the truth. It is to your advantage that I go away; for if I do not go away, the Helper will not come to you; but if I depart, I will send Him to you. And when He has come, He will convict the world of sin, and of righteousness, and of judgment... [John 16: 7 – 8]

Now when they heard this, they were cut to the heart, and said to Peter and the rest of the apostles, "Men and brethren, what shall we do?" Then Peter said to them, "Repent, and let every one of you be baptized in the name of Jesus Christ for the remission of sins; and you shall receive the gift of the Holy Spirit. [Acts 2:37, 38]

- **The Holy Spirit saves us by giving us new birth into the Kingdom of God!**
  In Him you also trusted, after you heard the word of truth, the gospel of your salvation; in whom also, having believed, you were sealed with the Holy Spirit of promise... [Ephesians 1:13]

  Not by works of righteousness which we have done, but according to His mercy He saved us, through the washing of regeneration and renewing of the Holy Spirit... [Titus 3:5]

- **The Holy Spirit transforms us so that we can cultivate the fruit of Christ's Character!**
  Now the Lord is the Spirit; and where the Spirit of the Lord is, there is liberty. But we all, with unveiled face, beholding as in a mirror the glory of the Lord, are being transformed

into the same image from glory to glory, just as by the Spirit of the Lord. [2 Corinthians 3:17, 18,]

*But the fruit of the Spirit is love, joy, peace, longsuffering, kindness, goodness, faithfulness, **gentleness**, self-control. Against such there is no law. And those who are Christ's have crucified the flesh with its passions and desires. If we live in the Spirit, let us also walk in the Spirit. Let us not become conceited, provoking one another, envying one another.* [Galatians 5:22 – 26]

- **The Holy Spirit empowers us with gifts so that we can manifest the Ministry of Christ!**
  "Most assuredly, I say to you, he who believes in Me, the works that I do he will do also; and greater works than these he will do, because I go to My Father... But you shall receive power when the Holy Spirit has come upon you; and you shall be witnesses to Me in Jerusalem, and in all Judea and Samaria, and to the end of the earth." [John 14:12, Acts 1:8]

There are diversities of gifts, but the same Spirit. But the manifestation of the Spirit is given to each one for the profit of all: for to one is given the word of wisdom through the Spirit, to another the word of knowledge through the same Spirit, to another faith by the same Spirit, to another gifts of healings by the same Spirit, to another the working of miracles, to another prophecy, to another discerning of spirits, to another different kinds of tongues, to another the interpretation of tongues. But one and the same Spirit works all these things, distributing to each one individually as He wills. [1 Corinthians 12:4, 7 – 11]

- **We will receive the fullness of the Holy Spirit's power if we ask the Father for Him in sincere faith!**

  This only I want to learn from you: Did you receive the Spirit by the works of the law, or by the hearing of faith? [Galatians 3:2]

  "So I say to you, ask, and it will be given to you; seek, and you will find; knock, and it will be opened to you. For everyone who asks receives, and he who seeks finds, and to him who knocks it will be opened. If a son asks for bread from any father among you, will he give him a stone? Or if he asks for a fish, will he give him a serpent instead of a fish? Or if he asks for an egg, will he offer him a scorpion? If you then, being evil, know how to give good gifts to your children, how much more will your heavenly Father give the Holy Spirit to those who ask Him!" [Luke 11:9 – 13]

Reflective Questions

Answer the following questions giving reasons where necessary

1. Have you been building a close relationship of sensitivity, submission and obedience to the Holy Spirit?

   _____

   _____

   _____

   _____

   _____

2. List the components of the fruit of the Holy Spirit. Have you been cultivating these in your life?

   _____

   _____

   _____

   _____

   _____

3. Have you asked God in faith for the fullness of the Holy Spirit since you became a disciple of Christ? Do you want to ask Him now?

   _____

   _____

   _____

   _____

   _____

CHAPTER TWELVE

WITNESS

But ye shall receive power, after that the Holy Ghost is come upon you: and ye shall be witnesses unto me both in Jerusalem, and in all Judaea, and in Samaria, and unto the uttermost part of the earth. [Acts 1:8]

Witness

A witness is one who *has a testimony to share of something he has experienced whether seen or heard*! The Apostles of Christ were eyewitnesses of the life, teachings, miracles, death, burial and resurrection of Christ and they were willing to die for it! That is why we can trust their testimony about Him written in the Bible — the Word of God! We can also become witnesses of the Word of God through our consistent daily walk with the Holy Spirit. As we walk faithfully with Him we will experience His reality and hence garner testimonies of what he has done or is doing in our lives!

Here are some important things about witnessing:

- **Every witness must have and be willing to share his testimony!**
  That which was from the beginning, which we have heard, which we have seen with our eyes, which we have looked upon, and our hands have handled, concerning the Word of life— the life was manifested, and we have seen, and bear witness, and declare to you that eternal life which was with the Father and was manifested to us— that which we have seen and heard we declare to you, that you also may have fellowship with us; and truly our fellowship is with the Father and with His Son Jesus Christ.
  [1 John 1:1 – 3]

  For we cannot but speak the things which we have seen and heard." [Acts 4:20]

- **We must be actively prepared and trained to become effective witnesses of the Lord Jesus Christ!**
  Be diligent to present yourself approved to God, a worker who does not need to be ashamed, rightly dividing the word of truth. [2 Timothy 2:15]

  But even if you should suffer for righteousness' sake, you are blessed. "And do not be afraid of their threats, nor be troubled." But sanctify the Lord God in your hearts, and always be ready to give a defense to everyone who asks you a reason for the hope that is in you, with meekness and fear... [1 Peter 3:14, 15]

- **Sharing our testimony about what God has done in our lives empowers us to grow in God and to defeat the enemy!**

  That the sharing of your faith may become effective by the acknowledgment of every good thing which is in you in Christ Jesus. [Philemon 1:6]

  And they overcame him by the blood of the Lamb and by the word of their testimony, and they did not love their lives to the death. [Revelations 12:11]

- **We should expect opposition and persecution for sharing our faith and testimony about what God has done for us!**

  So they called them and commanded them not to speak at all nor teach in the name of Jesus. But Peter and John answered and said to them, "Whether it is right in the sight of God to listen to you more than to God, you judge. For we cannot but speak the things which we have seen and heard. [Acts 4:18 – 20]

  Yes, and all who desire to live godly in Christ Jesus will suffer persecution. [2 Timothy 3:12]

- **The Holy Spirit equips us with power to enforce our witness about God and His Kingdom!**

  But you shall receive power when the Holy Spirit has come upon you; and you shall be witnesses to Me in Jerusalem, and in all Judea and Samaria, and to the end of the earth." [Acts 1:8]

And with great power the apostles gave witness to the resurrection of the Lord Jesus. And great grace was upon them all. [Acts 4:33]

And they went out and preached everywhere, the Lord working with them and confirming the word through the accompanying signs. Amen. [Mark 16:20]

Reflective Questions

Answer the following questions giving reasons where necessary

1. Have you been a true and faithful witness of Christ lately? How would you rate your personal witness for Christ out of 10?

   _____

   _____

   _____

   _____

   _____

2. What do you think are some of the hindrances to you becoming a faithful and effective witness for Christ? And how do you think you can overcome these obstacles?

   _____

   _____

   _____

   _____

   _____

3. How do you think being baptized with the Holy Spirit will enhance your witnessing experience?

   _____

   _____

   _____

   _____

   _____

Made in the USA
Columbia, SC
15 February 2025

53867654R00037